PIANO • VOCAL • GUITAR

THE FISH SERIES

WORSHIP
THE BEST OF CONTEMPORARY CHRISTIAN MUSIC

ISBN 978-1-4234-5640-7

HAL•LEONARD® CORPORATION

7777 W. BLUEMOUND RD. P.O. BOX 13819 MILWAUKEE, WI 53213

Visit Hal Leonard Online at
www.halleonard.com

ABOVE ALL

Words and Music by PAUL BALOCHE
and LENNY LeBLANC

AMAZED

Words and Music by
JARED ANDERSON

Moderately slow

You dance _ o - ver me _ while I _ am un - a - ware. _

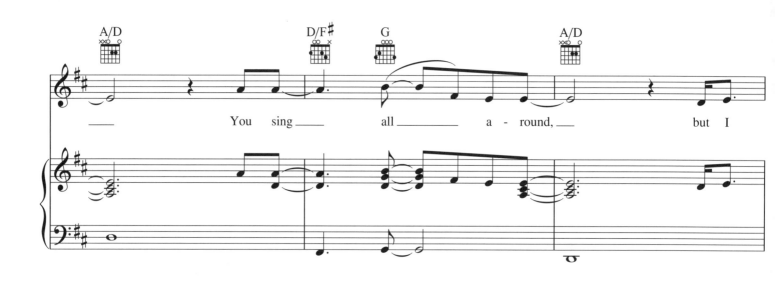

_ You sing _ all _ a - round, _ but I

nev - er hear _ the sound. _ Lord, I'm a - mazed _ by You. _

Recorded a half step lower.

AMAZING GRACE
(My Chains Are Gone)

Words by JOHN NEWTON
Traditional American Melody
Additional Words and Music by CHRIS TOMLIN
and LOUIE GIGLIO

shine. But God, who called me here be-low will

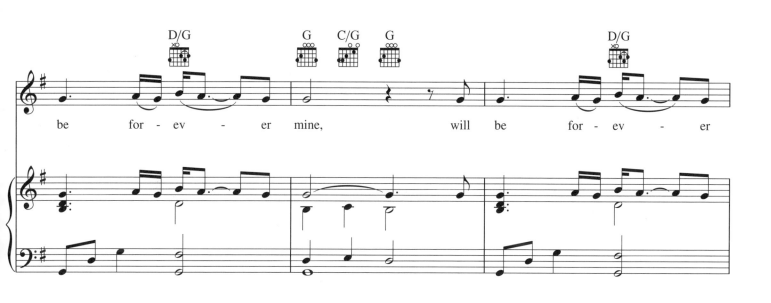

be for - ev - er mine, will be for - ev - er

mine. You are for - ev - er mine.

rit.

AT THE CROSS

Words and Music by REUBEN MORGAN
and DARLENE ZSCHECH

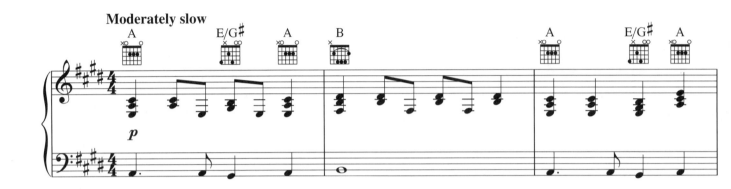

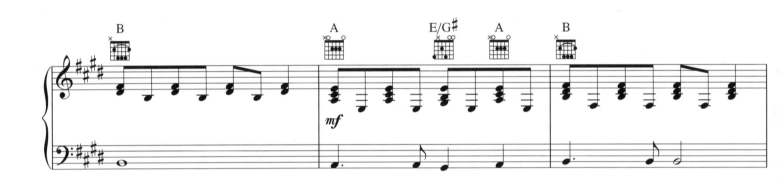

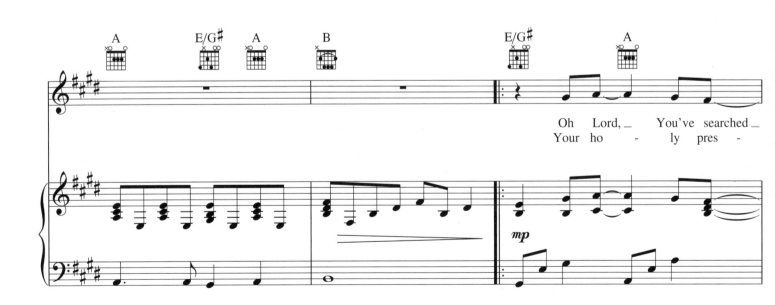

Oh Lord, __ You've searched __
Your ho - ly pres -

BECAUSE OF YOUR LOVE

Words and Music by PAUL BALOCHE
and BRENTON BROWN

Yeah, _____ yeah. _____ As we come in-to _____ Your pres - ence, _____ we re-

BEAUTIFUL ONE

Words and Music by
TIM HUGHES

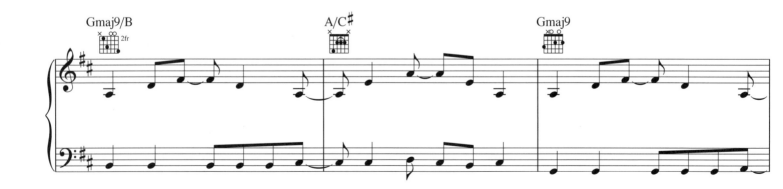

COME THOU FOUNT, COME THOU KING

Traditional
Additional Words and Music by
THOMAS MILLER

With movement

Come Thou _ Fount of ev-'ry

lost in ut-ter

grace, how great a

bless-ing, tune my heart to sing Thy _ grace. Streams of _
dark-ness till You came and res-cued _ me. I was _
debt-or dai-ly I'm con-strained to _ be. Let Thy _

mer-cy, nev-er ceas-ing, call for songs of loud-est _
bound by all my sin when Your love came and set me _
good-ness, like a fet-ter, bind my wan-d'ring heart to _

FOR WHO YOU ARE

Words and Music by
MARTY SAMPSON

With energy

*Recorded a half step lower.

for who __ You are, Je - sus. __

I will wor-ship You __

Guitar solo ad lib.

CONSUMING FIRE

Words and Music by
TIM HUGHES

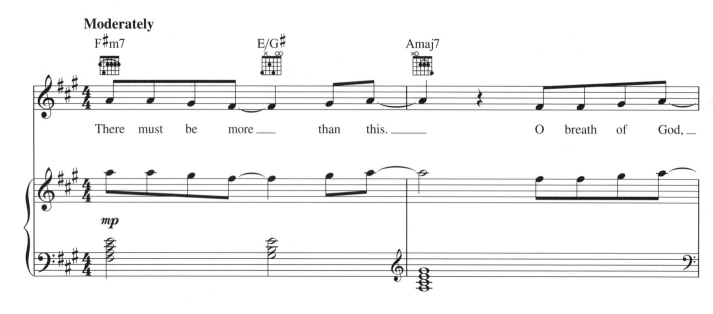

There must be more ___ than this. ___ O breath of God, ___

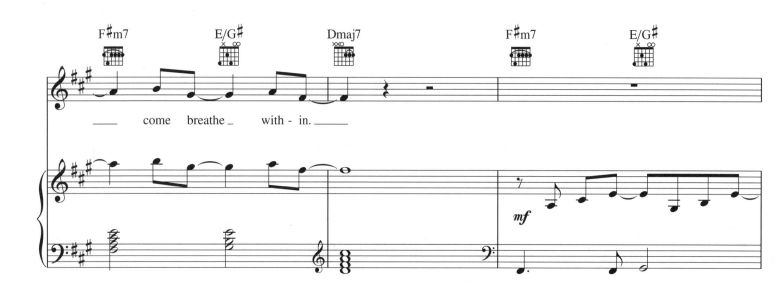

___ come breathe ___ with - in. ___

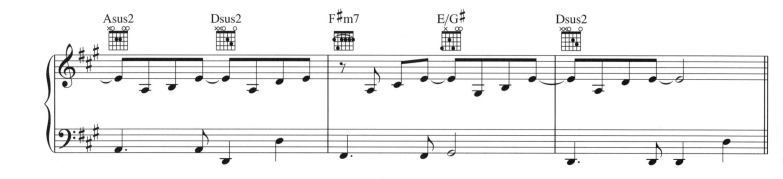

50

Come like a rush - ing wind, ___ clothe us with pow - er from ___ on high. ___

___ Now set the cap - tives free. ___ Leave us a - ban -

- doned to ___ Your praise. ___ Lord, let Your glo - ry fall. ___

___ O ___ Lord, let Your glo - ry fall. ___ Con - sum - ing

D.S. al Coda

DAYS OF ELIJAH

Words and Music by
ROBIN MARK

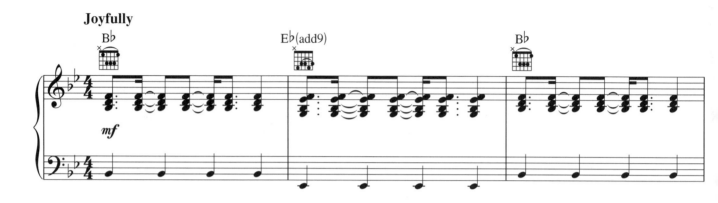

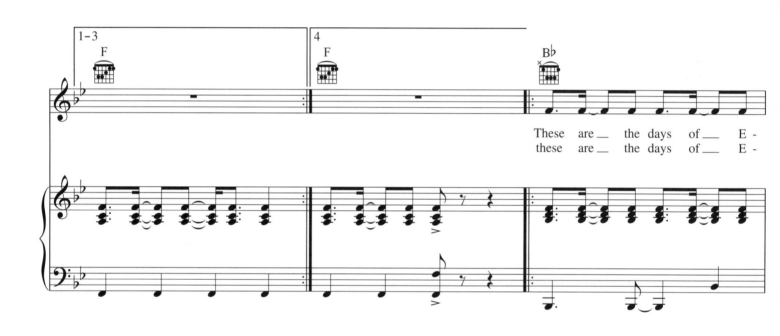

These are __ the days of __ E-
these are __ the days of __ E-

li - jah, __ de - clar - ing __ the Word of __ the Lord. And
ze - kiel, __ the dry bones __ be - com - ing __ as flesh. And

ENOUGH

Words and Music by CHRIS TOMLIN
and LOUIE GIGLIO

Steadily

All of You ___ is more than e - nough ___

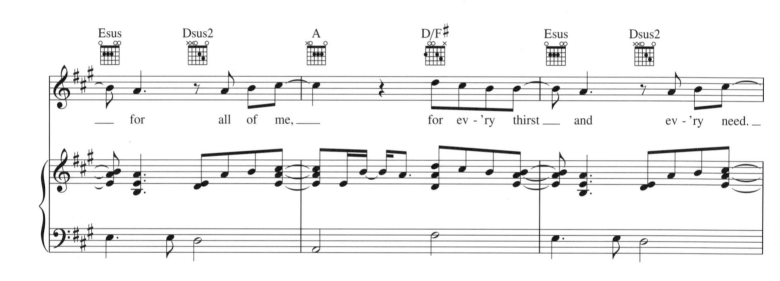

___ for all of me, ___ for ev - 'ry thirst ___ and ev - 'ry need. ___

___ You ___ sat - is - fy ___ me with Your love, ___ and all I have ___ in You ___

FOREVER

Words and Music by
CHRIS TOMLIN

FRIEND OF GOD

Words and Music by MICHAEL GUNGOR
and ISRAEL HOUGHTON

Moderate Rock beat

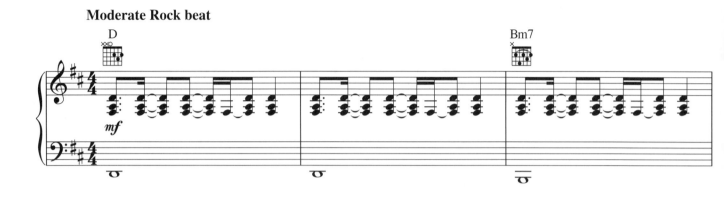

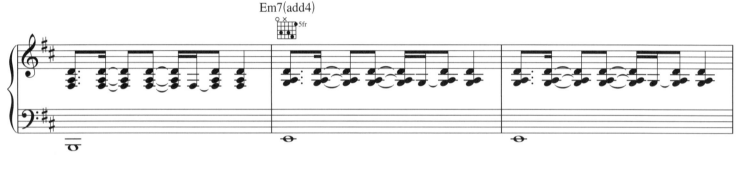

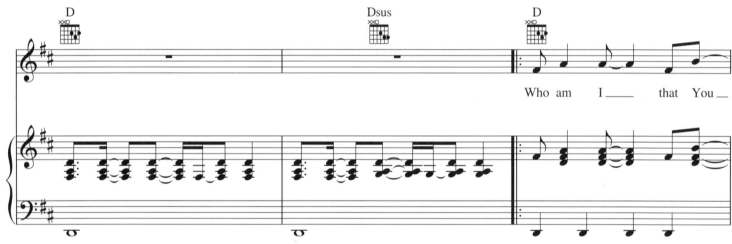

Who am I ___ that You ___

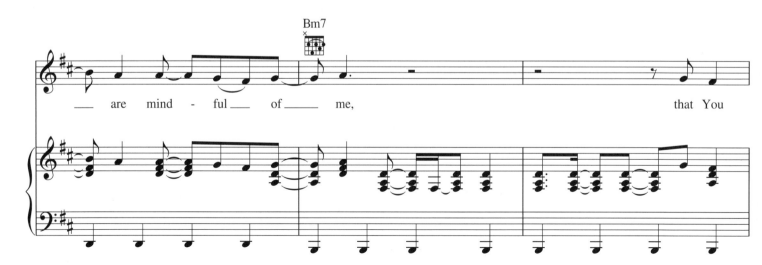

___ are mind-ful ___ of ___ me,   that You

FROM THE INSIDE OUT

Words and Music by
JOEL HOUSTON

Worshipfully

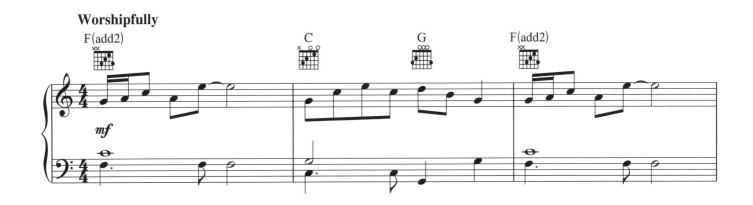

(1.) A thou-sand times _ I've _ failed, _ still Your mer-
(2.,3.) bove _ all _ else _ my pur-

-cy re-mains. _ And should I stum-ble a- gain, _ I'm caught _
-pose re-mains, _ the art of los-ing my-self _ in bring-

In my heart and my soul, ___ well, I give You con-trol. ___ Con-sume me from the

in - side out, Lord. Let jus - tice and praise ___ be - come my em - brace, _

cresc. poco a poco

___ to love You from the in - side out. Ev - er - last - ing, Your light will shine when

all else fades. Nev - er - end - ing, Your glo - ry goes be - yond all fame. And the cry _

_____ of my heart _____ is to bring _____ You praise. From the in -

- side out, Lord, my soul _____ cries out. Ev - er - last - _____ cries out, from the in -

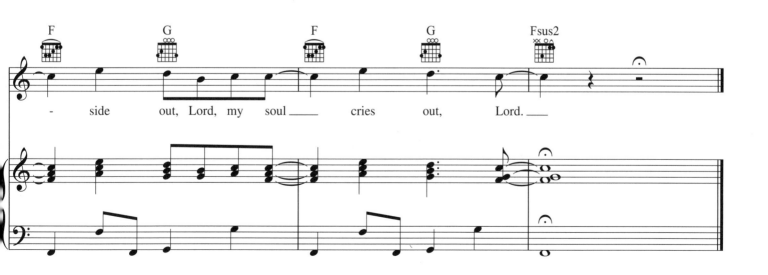

- side out, Lord, my soul _____ cries out, Lord. _____

GLORIOUS

Words and Music by CHRIS TOMLIN
and JESSE REEVES

GRACE FLOWS DOWN

Words and Music by LOUIE GIGLIO,
DAVID BELL and ROD PADGETT

HEAR OUR PRAISES

Words and Music by
REUBEN MORGAN

May our homes ___ be filled ___ with danc - ing, ___
May our light ___ shine in ___ the dark - ness ___

may our streets ___ be filled ___ with joy, ___
as we walk ___ be - fore ___ the cross. ___

Hal - le - lu - jah, _____ hal - le -

HERE I AM TO WORSHIP

Words and Music by
TIM HUGHES

Light of the World, You stepped down in-to dark - ness,
King of all days, oh so high - ly ex - alt - ed,

o - pened my eyes, let me _____ see. ___ Beau - ty that made this ___
glo - rious in heav - en a - bove. ___ Hum - bly You came to the

heart a - dore ___ You, hope of a life spent with ___ You. ___
earth You cre - a - ted, all for love's sake be - came ___ poor. ___

- er know_ how much_ it cost_ to see_____ my sin_ up - on_

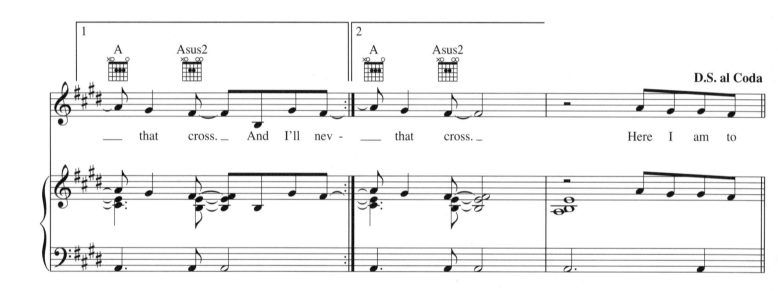

1

__ that cross._ And I'll nev - __ that cross._

2

Here I am to

D.S. al Coda

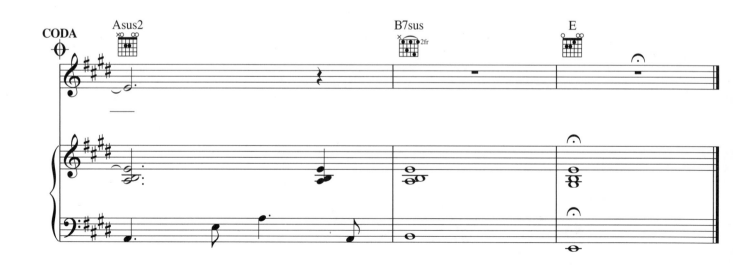

CODA

MARVELOUS LIGHT

Words and Music by
CHARLIE HALL

With praise

Into mar-vel-ous light I'm run-ning,

out of dark-ness, out of shame. By the cross You

are the truth, You are the life, You are the way. _____

Recorded a half step lower.

I once was fa - ther - less, a stran - ger ___ with no hope.

HERE IS OUR KING

Words and Music by
DAVID CROWDER

Here is our King, here is our Love, here is our God who's come to bring us back to Him. He is the One, He is Je - sus. And He is our

HOLY IS THE LORD

Words and Music by CHRIS TOMLIN
and LOUIE GIGLIO

HOW DEEP THE FATHER'S LOVE FOR US

Words and Music by
STUART TOWNEND

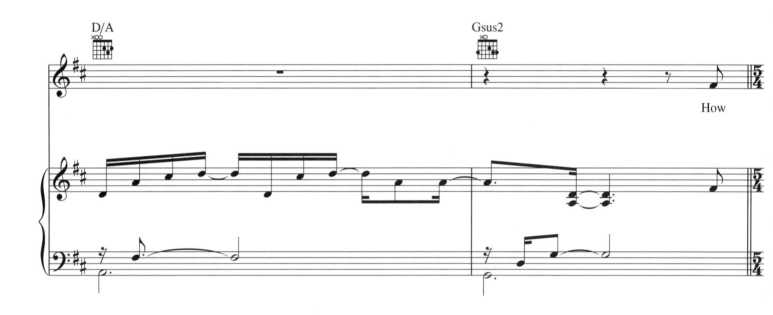

deep the Fa-ther's love for us; how vast be-yond all meas-ure that
hold the man up-on a cross, my sin up-on His shoul-ders. A-
will not boast in an-y-thing, no gifts, no pow'r, no wis-dom, but

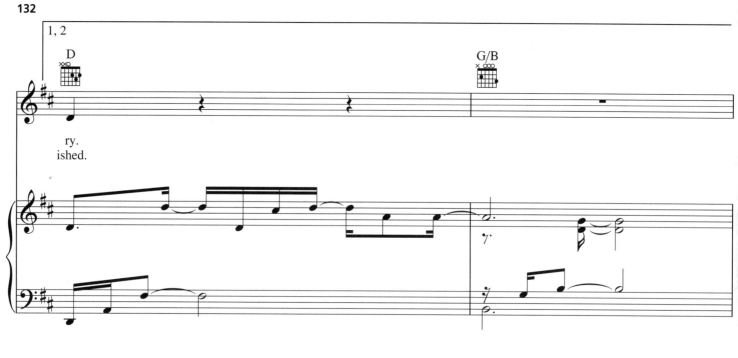

ry.
ished.

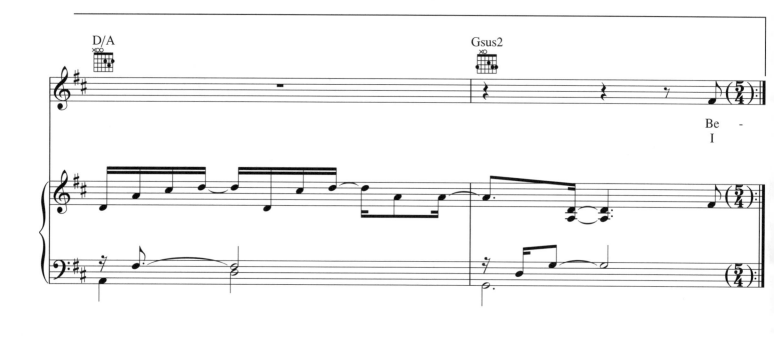

Be -
I

som.   Why should I gain from His re - ward?   I

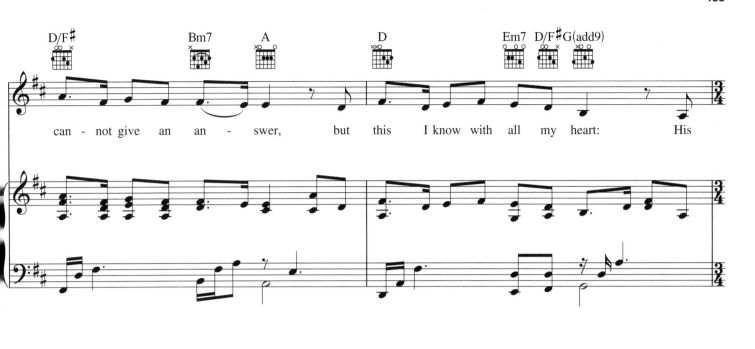

can - not give an an - swer, but this I know with all my heart: His

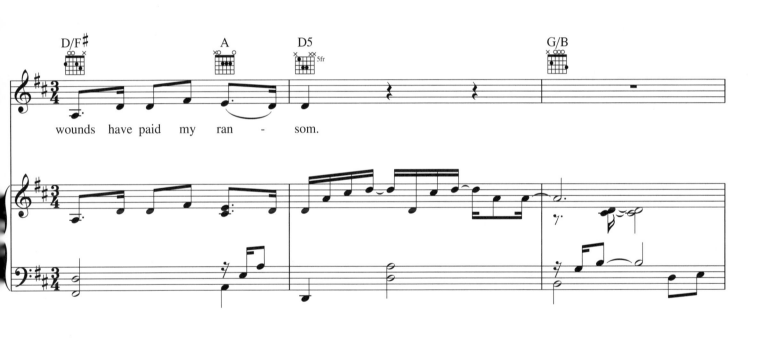

wounds have paid my ran - som.

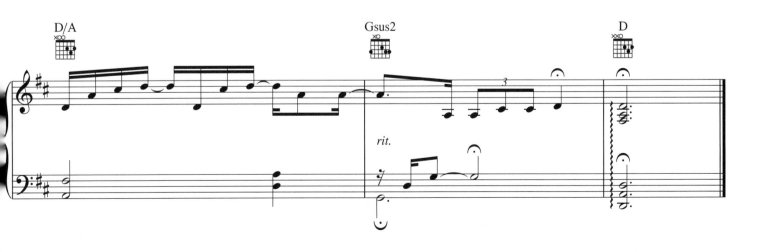

I AM FREE

Words and Music by
JON EGAN

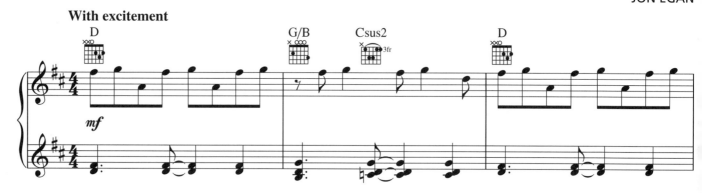

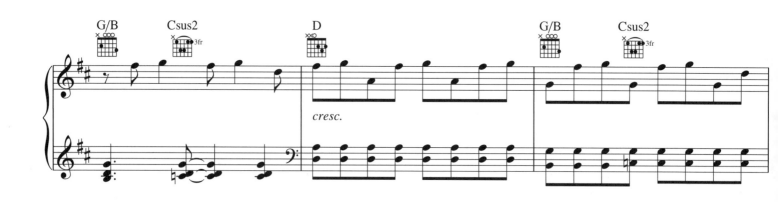

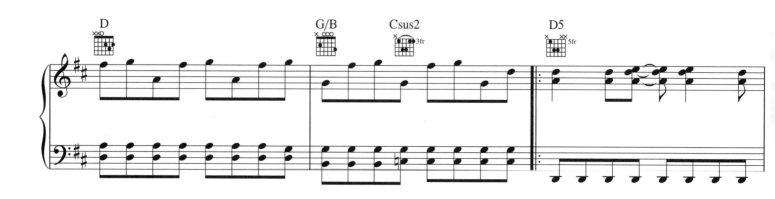

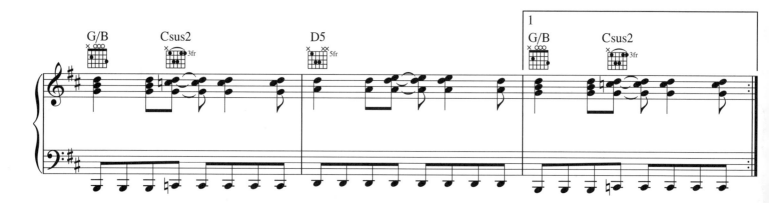

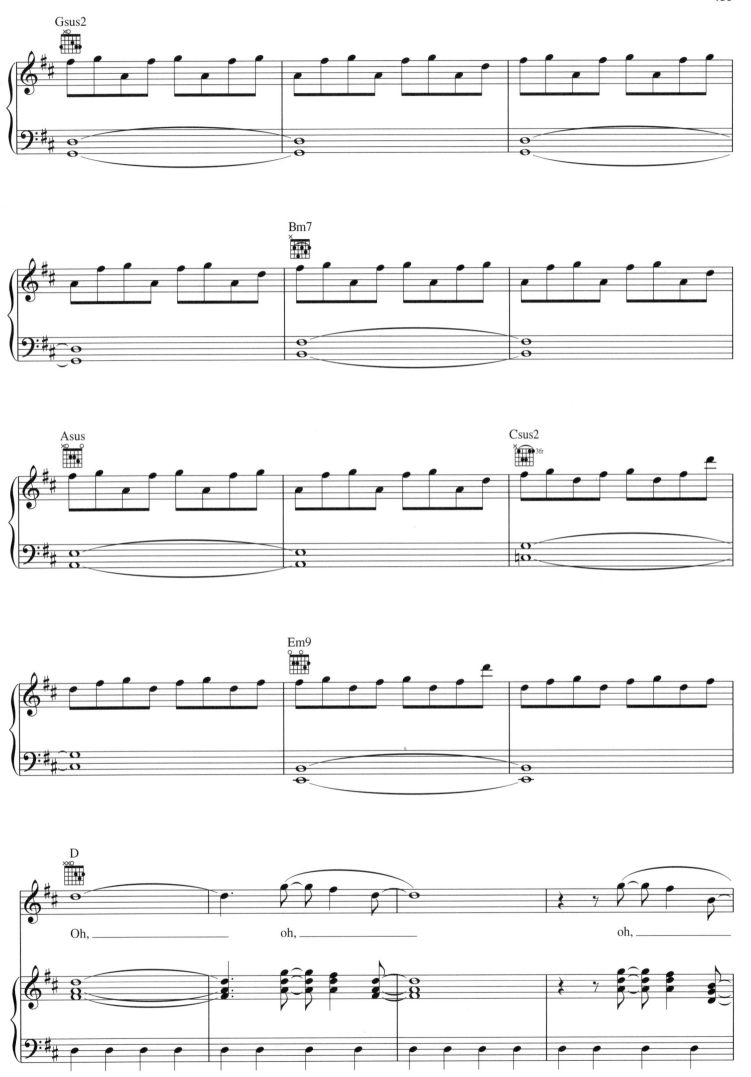

IN CHRIST ALONE

Words and Music by KEITH GETTY
and STUART TOWNEND

LET THE PRAISES RING

Words and Music by
LINCOLN BREWSTER

Let the prais - es _____ ring!

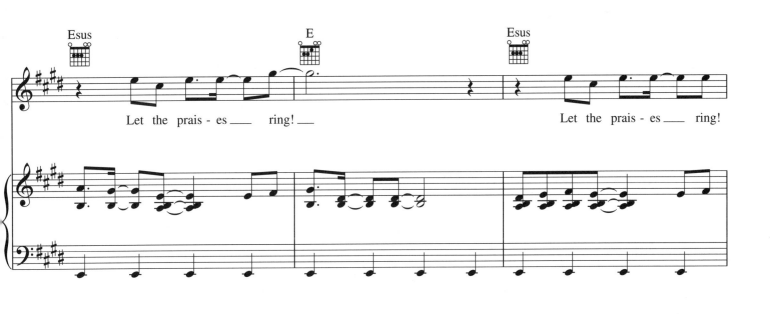

Let the prais - es _____ ring! _____   Let the prais - es _____ ring!

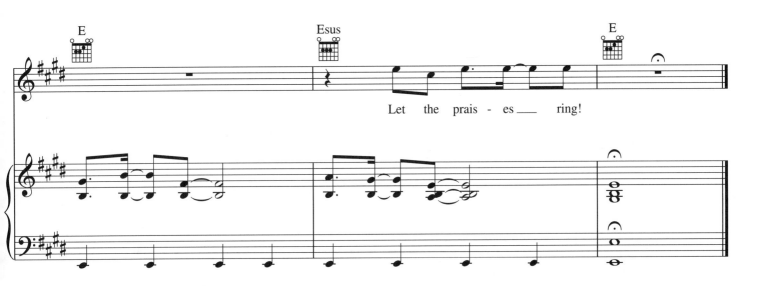

Let the prais - es _____ ring!

MIGHTY TO SAVE

Words and Music by BEN FIELDING
and REUBEN MORGAN

MY GLORIOUS

Words and Music by MARTIN SMITH
and STUART GARRARD

MY SAVIOR LIVES

Words and Music by JON EGAN
and GLENN PACKIAM

Driving Rock

Our God will reign _____ for - ev - er, and all the world_
The King has come _____ from Heav - en, and dark - ness trem -

_____ will know His name. _____ Ev - 'ry - one _____ to - geth - er,
- bles at His name. _____ Vic - to - ry _____ for - ev - er

Recorded a half step lower.

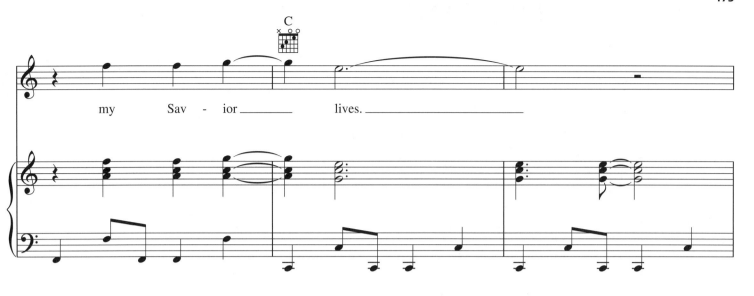

my Sav - ior _____ lives. _____

My Sav - ior, my Sav - ior _____ lives.

My Sav - ior, my Sav - ior lives.

NO ONE LIKE YOU

Words and Music by JACK PARKER, MIKE DODSON,
JASON SOLLEY, MIKE HOGAN,
JEREMY BUSH and DAVID CROWDER

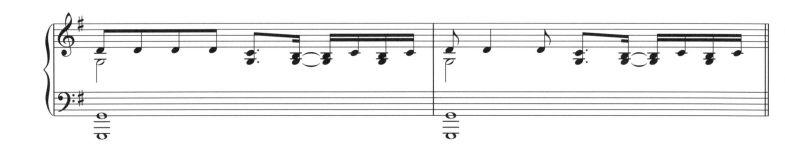

You are more beau - ti - ful than an - y - one ev - er.

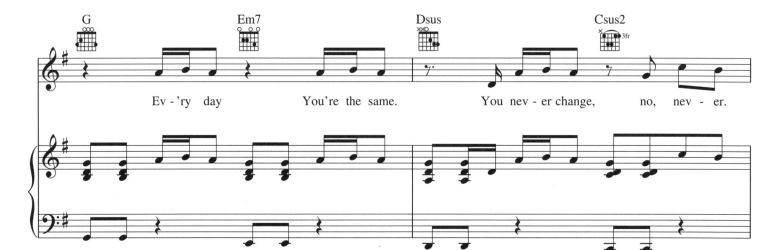

Ev - 'ry day You're the same. You nev - er change, no, nev - er.

*Recorded a half step lower.

NONE BUT JESUS

Words and Music by
BROOKE FRASER

Cru - ci - fied to set me ___ free, ___ now I live ___

1
___ to bring Him praise.

2
___ to bring Him praise.

And all my de - light ___ is in ___ You, Lord, ___

___ all of my ___ hope ___ and all of my ___ strength. ___

NOT TO US

Words and Music by CHRIS TOMLIN
and JESSE REEVES

*Recorded a half step lower.

NOTHING BUT THE BLOOD

Words and Music by
MATT REDMAN

*Recorded a half step lower.

O PRAISE HIM
(All This for a King)

Words and Music by
DAVID CROWDER

Moderately fast

PROMISES

Words and Music by
JARED ANDERSON

Up-tempo Rock

All of Your prom-is-es won't let go ___ of me.

(All of Your prom-is-es won't let go ___ of me.)

I've sur-ren-dered my life ___ to Your ways, ___

ONE WAY

Words and Music by JOEL HOUSTON
and JONATHON DOUGLASS

With a driving beat

Lyrics:

I lay my life down __
You are al - ways, __
at Your feet.
al - ways there,
You're the on - ly One I need.
ev - 'ry "how" and ev - 'ry "where."

Recorded a half step lower.

Je - sus. You're the on - ly one that I could live ___ for.

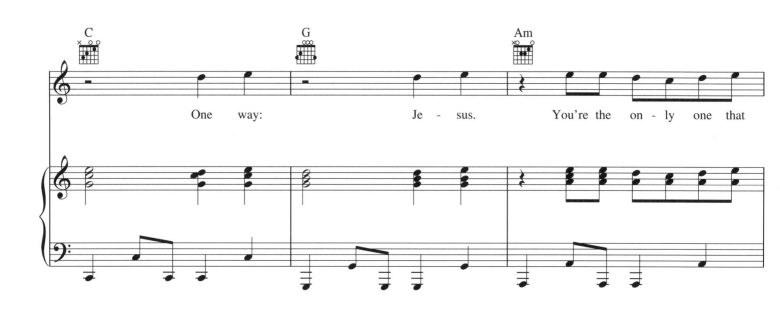

One way: Je - sus. You're the on - ly one that

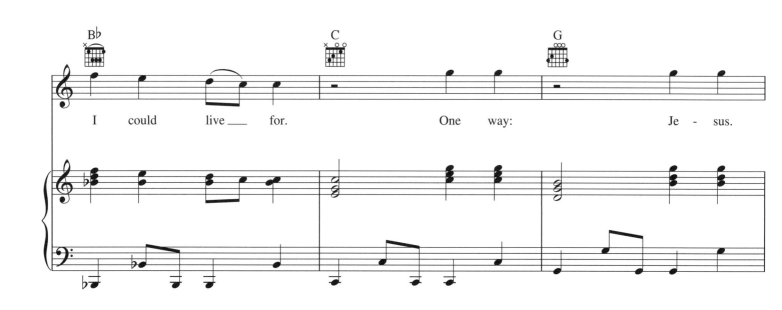

I could live ___ for. One way: Je - sus.

You're the on-ly one that I could live ___ for. One way:

Je - sus. You're the on-ly one that I could live ___ for, ___

___ I could live for. _____

REVELATION SONG

Words and Music by
JENNIE LEE RIDDLE

With praise

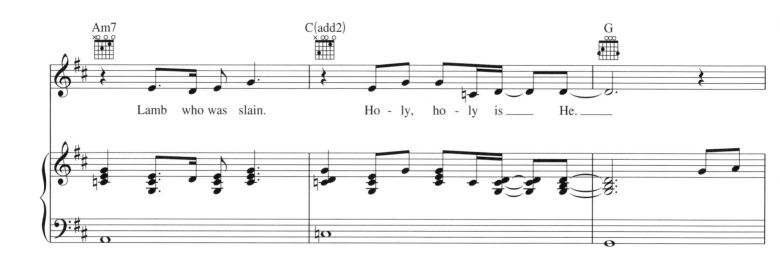

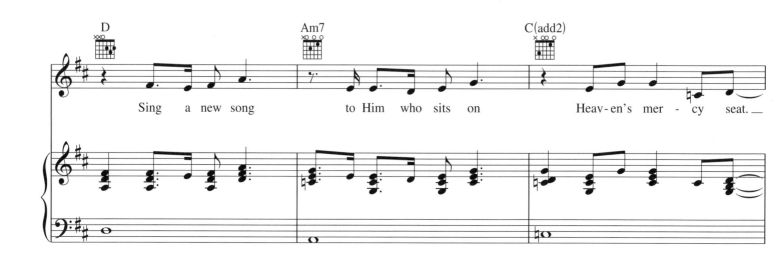

REVIVAL

Words and Music by
ROBIN MARK

With energy

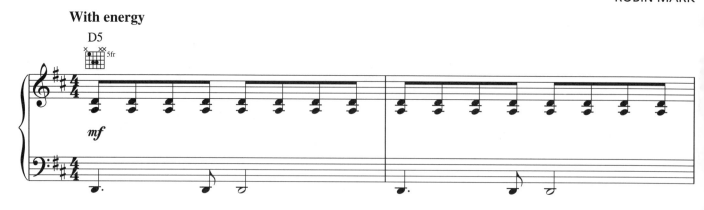

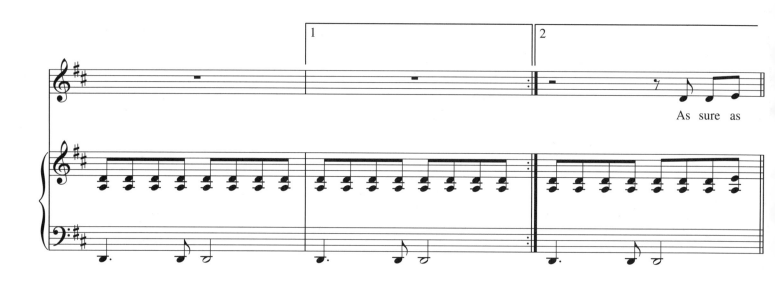

As sure as

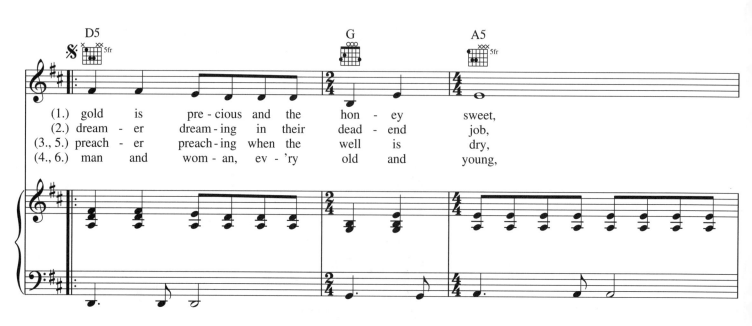

(1.) gold is pre-cious and the hon-ey sweet,
(2.) dream-er dream-ing in their dead-end job,
(3., 5.) preach-er preach-ing when the well is dry,
(4., 6.) man and wom-an, ev-'ry old and young,

so You love this cit - y and You love these
ev - 'ry driv - er driv - ing through the rush - hour
to the lost soul reach - ing for a high - er
ev - 'ry fa - ther's daugh - ter, ev - 'ry moth - er's

streets.
mob,
high.
son.

Ev - 'ry child out play - ing by their
I feel it in my spir - it, feel it
From the young man work - ing through his
I feel it in my spir - it, feel it

own front door,
in my bones,
hopes and fears,
in my bones,

ev - 'ry
You're gon - na
to the
You're gon - na

feel the brood-ing of Your Spir - it, "Lay your bur - dens

down, lay your bur - dens down."

3. From the

Re - vive

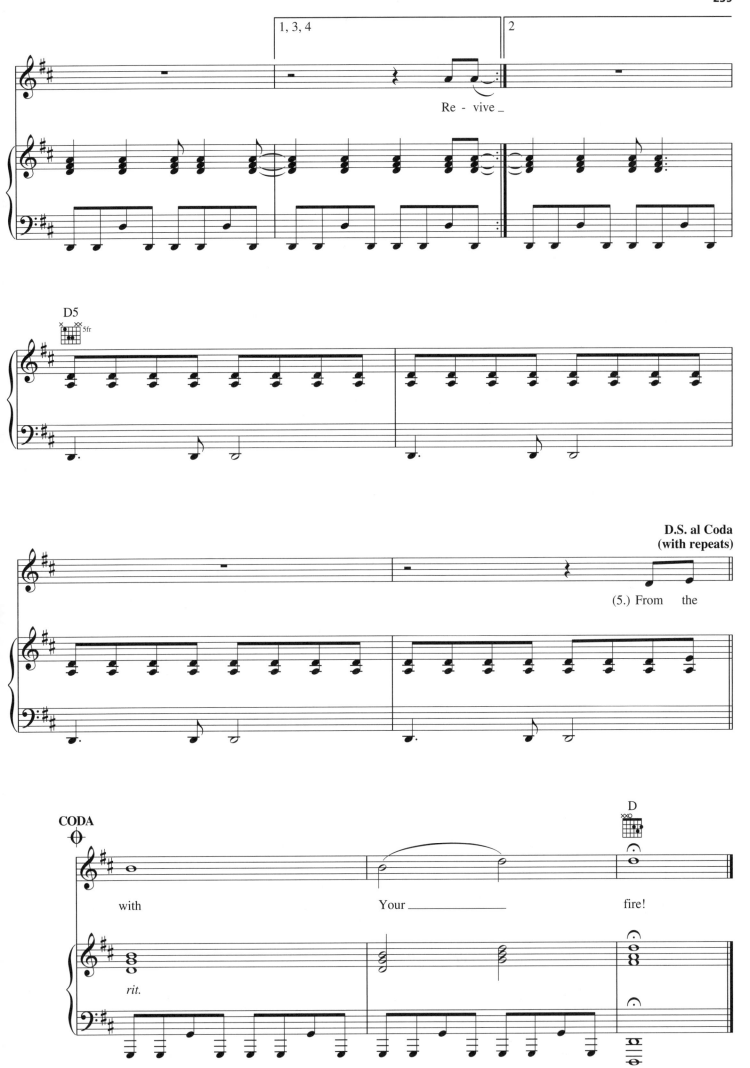

RISING

Words and Music by PAUL BALOCHE
and MATT REDMAN

Joyfully

From the ris- ing of the sun till the sun____

____ goes down,_ let the name ___ of the Lord be praised. _ From the ris-

- ing of the sun till the sun___ goes down,_ let the name ___ of the Lord_ be praised. _

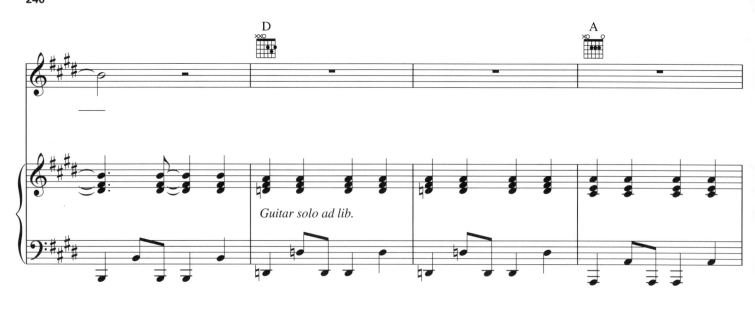

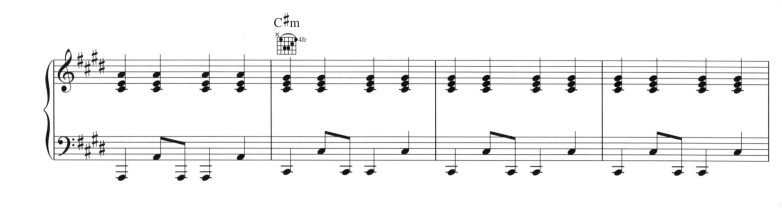

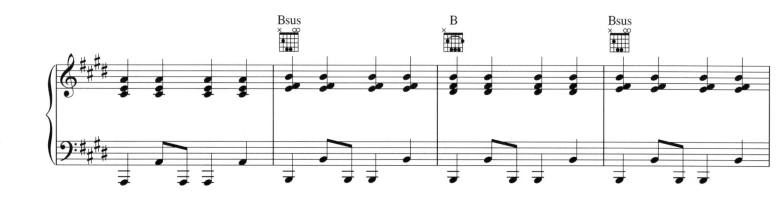

SHOUT TO THE NORTH

Words and Music by
MARTIN SMITH

With a lilt

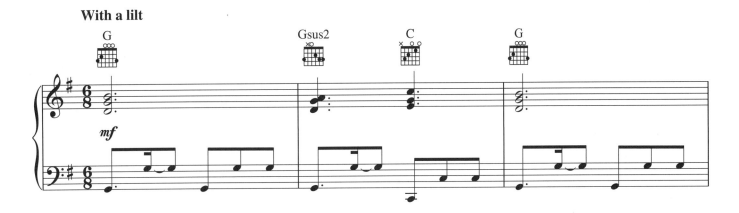

Men of faith, rise __ up and __
wom - en __ of the __
church with __ bro - ken __

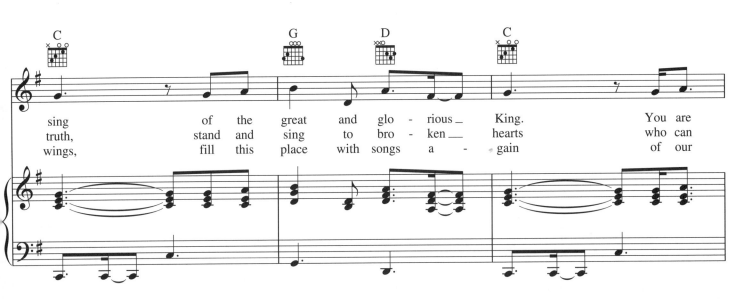

sing   of the great and glo - rious __ King.   You are
truth,   stand and sing to bro - ken __ hearts   who can
wings,   fill this place with songs a - gain   of our

SAY SO

Words and Music by MICHAEL GUNGOR
and ISRAEL HOUGHTON

High energy

What does it mean ___ to be saved? ___ Is - n't it more ___ oh, that we ___
Oh, that the church ___ will a - rise, ___

___ than just ___ a prayer ___ to pray, ___ more ___
___ would see ___ with Je - sus' eyes; ___ we ___

___ than just ___ a way ___ to heav - en? ___
___ could just show ___ the world ___ heav - en. ___

SING TO THE KING

Words and Music by
BILLY JAMES FOOTE

Life and sal - va - tion His em - pire shall bring,
We'll join in sing - ing with all the re - deemed,

and joy to the na - tions when
'cause Sa - tan is van - quished and

Je - sus is King.
Je - sus is King.

1

2, 3

Come, let us sing a song, a

SONG OF LOVE

Words and Music by REBECCA ST. JAMES,
MATT BRONLEEWE and JEREMY ASH

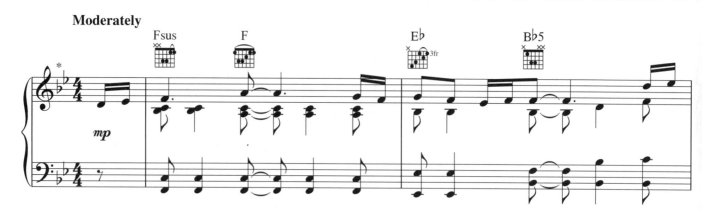

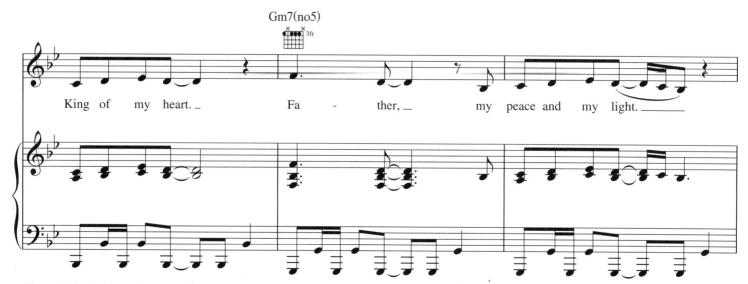

Recorded a half step higher.

THANK YOU, LORD

Words and Music by PAUL BALOCHE
and DON MOEN

SWEETER

Words and Music by CINDY CRUSE-RATCLIFF,
ISRAEL HOUGHTON and MELEASA HOUGHTON

UNCHANGING

Words and Music by
CHRIS TOMLIN

Great is ____ Your faith - ful - ness, ____

great is ____ Your faith - ful - ness. ____

WE ALL BOW DOWN

Words and Music by
LENNY LeBLANC

CODA

He is the love __ of God. __ He's the Light of __ the world, __ and Lord of __ the cross. __ And we all bow down. __ Kings will sur-ren-der their crowns __ and wor - ship __ Je -

YOU ARE GOD ALONE
(not a god)

Words and Music by BILLY J. FOOTE
and CINDY FOOTE

You are not a

god cre - at - ed by hu - man hands. __

Recorded a half step lower.

un - stop - pa - ble, _____ that's what You are. _____

WE GIVE YOU GLORY

Words and Music by
JEREMY CAMP

WONDERFUL MAKER

Words and Music by MATT REDMAN
and CHRIS TOMLIN

You spread out the skies o-ver emp-ty space.

Said, "Let there be light," and to a dark and form-less world Your light

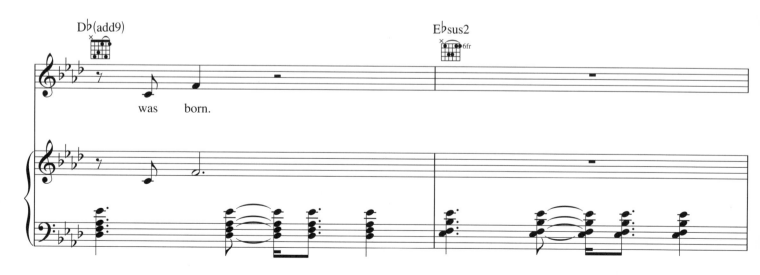

was born.

YOU, YOU ARE GOD

Words and Music by
MICHAEL WALKER BEACH

THE FISH SERIES

THE BEST OF CONTEMPORARY CHRISTIAN MUSIC

The ancient Greek "sign of the fish" (Ichthys) is an instantly recognizable Christian symbol in pop culture. It is used on car bumpers, clothing, jewelry, business logos, and more. Hal Leonard is proud to offer The Fish Series, showcasing the wide variety of music styles that comprise the Contemporary Christian genre. From the early pioneers of CCM to today's biggest hits, there's something for everyone!

CHRISTMAS (Green Book)
40 Contemporary Christian holiday favorites, including: Christmas Angels • Christmas Is All in the Heart • He Made a Way in a Manger • Joseph's Lullaby • Manger Throne • Not That Far from Bethlehem • 2000 Decembers Ago • While You Were Sleeping • and more.
00311755 P/V/G..................................$19.95

EARLY YEARS (Orange Book)
41 songs, including: The Day He Wore My Crown • Father's Eyes • I Wish We'd All Been Ready • Love Crucified Arose • Rise Again • Sing Your Praise to the Lord • Who Will Save the Children • Your Love Broke Through • and more.
00311756 P/V/G..................................$21.95

INSPIRATIONAL (Blue Book)
42 songs of encouragement and exaltation, including: Call on Jesus • Find Your Wings • God Will Make a Way • Healing Rain • Jesus Will Still Be There • On My Knees • Say the Name • Your Grace Still Amazes Me • and many more.
00311757 P/V/G..................................$19.95

POP (Red Book)
44 top pop hits from favorite Contemporary Christian artists, including: Always Have, Always Will • Brave • Circle of Friends • For Future Generations • If We Are the Body • Simple Things • To Ever Live Without Me • What It Means • and more.
00311758 P/V/G..................................$21.95

PRAISE (Yellow Book)
50 songs of praise and worship, including: Agnus Dei • Before the Throne of God Above • Come Just As You Are • He Knows My Name • Majesty • Open Our Eyes • Worthy of Worship • You Are My All in All • and many more.
00311759 P/V/G..................................$21.95

ROCK (Black Book)
41 rock hits from some of the biggest names in Contemporary Christian music, including: All Around Me • Count Me In • Everlasting God • I'm Not Alright • Meant to Live • No Matter What It Takes • Tunnel • Undo • and more.
00311760 P/V/G..................................$19.95

WEDDING (White Book)
40 songs from Contemporary Christian artists for the bride and groom's big day, including: Cinderella • God Knew That I Needed You • Household of Faith • I Will Be Here • Look What Love Has Done • A Page Is Turned • This Day • Without Love • and more.
00311761 P/V/G..................................$21.95

WORSHIP (Purple Book)
50 songs perfect for a worship band or solo praise, including: Amazing Grace (My Chains Are Gone) • Beautiful One • Days of Elijah • Forever • In Christ Alone • Mighty to Save • Revelation Song • Sing to the King • and many more.
00311762 P/V/G..................................$21.95

HAL•LEONARD® CORPORATION
7777 W. BLUEMOUND RD. P.O. BOX 13819 MILWAUKEE, WI 53213

Visit Hal Leonard Online at
www.halleonard.com

0808